Dad, Really!!

The Ultimate Teen and Dad Joke Book

M. S. Gregory

Copyright © 2025
by Tried and Trusted Indie Publishing

ISBN: 978-1-923623-10-1
All rights reserved.
Cover designed by msgdragon

No part of this publication may be reproduced, distributed, or transmitted in any form or by any means, including photocopying, recording, or other electronic or mechanical methods, without the prior written permission of the author, except non-commercial uses permitted by copyright law.

Also by M. S. Gregory

- Cousin Chaos: Laughing with your Cousins
- Sibling Shenanigans: Laughing with my Sister
- Sibling Shenanigans: Brother-Sister Jokes
- Mum Seriously!! Teen-mum banter at its finest!
- What Cats really Think: Hilarious Cat Thoughts, Jokes, and Conversations That Will Make You Laugh
- From Bark to Snark: Sassy thoughts from your Pup

For permission requests, address the request to the author c/o
Permissions,
TAT Indie Publishing
triedandtrustedindie@gmail.com

Dad: I tried to text you, but your phone was busy ignoring me. Must be a software feature called teen mode.

Dad: I asked you to clean your room, not start an archaeological dig.

Dad: You say you're "tired." From what — blinking at screens all day?

Dad: You think you're mysterious because you don't answer questions. You're not deep — you're just avoiding chores.

Dad: You say I'm old, but at least I didn't need a YouTube tutorial to boil pasta.

Dad: I saw your selfie. Nice confidence. Bold choice to use every filter but "reality."

Dad: Remember when you said you "don't do mornings"? Yeah, mornings feel the same way about you.

Dad: You say you're an adult now, but your laundry pile just applied for citizenship.

Dad: You call me old-fashioned, but I'm not the one using slang I don't understand five minutes later.

Dad: You said you'd be "ready in five minutes." Which timezone was that, exactly?

Teen: Dad, you're so embarrassing.
Dad: That's literally my job title.

Teen: Why do you always have to make jokes?
Dad: Because you make it too easy.

Teen: I'm not a kid anymore!
Dad: Great — then you can start paying rent.

Teen: You don't understand, Dad.
Dad: Oh, I understand. I just disagree. Big difference.

Teen: I can't wait to move out!
Dad: Same! I'll finally get Wi-Fi that works.

Teen: Why do you always check where I'm going?
Dad: Because last time, "five minutes" meant three hours and a new haircut.

Teen: You never let me do anything!
Dad: I let you breathe and eat my food — you're welcome.

Teen: You have no idea what it's like to be a teenager.
Dad: You're right. I was too busy walking uphill both ways.

Teen: Can you not talk to my friends, please?
Dad: Sure. I'll just yell from the car like last time.

Teen: Dad, you act like you're tech-savvy.
Dad: I am!
Teen: You once called Netflix "The YouTube Channel."

Teen: Dad, you're like a phone on 1% battery.
Dad: Meaning I'm running low?
Teen: Meaning you panic way too early.

Teen: You know what I admire about you, Dad?
Dad: What's that?
Teen: Your confidence in thinking cargo shorts are still in style.

Teen: Dad, your playlist is like ancient history.
Dad: Hey, those are classics!
Teen: So is the Roman Empire. Doesn't mean we should bring it back.

Teen: I told my friends you were on social media.
Dad: Yeah? What'd they say?
Teen: They said it explains why the algorithm's confused.

Teen: Dad, how do you always know when I'm about to do something dumb?
Dad: Experience.
Teen: Yeah, but you had to do those dumb things first, right?

Teen: You're like Wi-Fi, Dad.
Dad: Because I keep us connected?
Teen: Because you disappear right when I need you most.

Teen: I told my friends you're a "dad joke pro."
Dad: That's a compliment!
Teen: Yeah, but they thought it meant you're unemployed.

Teen: Dad, remember when you said you were "just resting your eyes"?
Dad: Yeah.
Teen: The snoring gave you away, big guy.

Teen: You say I'm addicted to my phone, but you talk to the TV during sports.
Dad: That's different.
Teen: Yeah, at least my phone sometimes listens.

Dad: You're spending your allowance online?
Teen: It's the future!
Dad: Back then, we earned a stick of gum and a pat on the back.

Teen: You know what's wild, Dad?
Dad: What?
Teen: How you drive like you're in a Fast & Furious movie… until someone asks to parallel park.

Teen: You're not old, Dad.
Dad: Thanks, kiddo.
Teen: You're just… retro. Like a museum exhibit that still mows lawns.

Teen: Dad, I love how confident you are.
Dad: Thanks!
Teen: Even when you're completely wrong — it's inspiring, really.

Teen: You've got that "dad bod" nailed.
Dad: Is that a compliment?
Teen: Sure — if comfort is a sport.

Teen: Dad, you're like my phone.
Dad: Always with you?
Teen: No, you start glitching after 9 p.m.

Teen: You're great at giving advice, Dad.
Dad: Thanks!
Teen: Now if only any of it applied to this century.

Teen: You say I spend too much time on my phone.
Dad: You do.
Teen: You spend 30 minutes talking to Alexa about the weather.

Teen: You know what I love most about you, Dad?
Dad: What's that?
Teen: You make me feel young... mostly by comparison

Teen: Dad, you're like my phone battery.
Dad: Always reliable?
Teen: No, you get tired by 9 p.m.

Dad: You have notifications for everything.
Teen Daughter: Keeps me organized.
Dad: Back then, we had sticky notes... and a lot of regret.

Dad: I walked 3 miles for ice cream.
Teen Daughter: I Uber there and complain it took 10 minutes.
Dad: Your legs aren't getting the same cardio, either.

Dad: We walked to school rain or shine.
Teen: Now I drive 3 minutes to school.
Dad: Lucky you — we built character one soggy sock at a time.

Dad: I read actual books.
Teen: I read memes.
Dad: At least your literacy is... emoji-literate.

Dad: We had to rewind VHS tapes manually.
Teen: We just click replay.
Dad: And call it patience, or convenience — depends on the era.

Dad: We didn't have autocorrect.
Teen: Now we have predictive text.
Dad: Which still fails spectacularly when you really need it.

Dad: You spend three hours on your phone?
Teen: It's homework… sort of.
Dad: Back in my day, we called that "being late for dinner."

Dad: You only drink iced coffee now?
Teen Daughter: It's a mood thing.
Dad: Back in my day, coffee was black, and mornings were hard. Now I see yours are just complicated.

Dad: You watch videos of cats all day?
Teen: They're educational.
Dad: Sure, if "how to ignore responsibility" counts as a skill.

Dad: You need a new phone every year?
Teen: Technology moves fast!
Dad: And yet somehow, your room hasn't moved an inch.

Dad: You're charging your tablet again?
Teen Daughter: Batteries die, Dad.
Dad: Back then, we just shouted until someone answered. Same result — attention.

Dad: You spend hours curating Instagram pictures?
Teen: It's called aesthetics.
Dad: Back in my day, we used film cameras and prayed we didn't ruin the roll. High stakes, low filters.[1]

1

Dad: You order food online every night?
Teen: It's easier.
Dad: Back then, "easier" meant walking to the store without whining.

Dad: You're late because of your headphones?
Teen Daughter: Music helps me focus!
Dad: Focused on what? Losing track of time again?

Dad: You text "LOL" but never laugh?
Teen: It's sarcasm, Dad.
Dad: Back in my day, sarcasm required vocal chords and eye rolls — harder, but more con-vincing.

Dad: You binge-watch an entire season in a day?
Teen Daughter: It's efficient.
Dad: Back then, we had to wait a week for the next episode — and learn patience... or fight with siblings over the remote.

Dad: You spend 30 minutes choosing a filter?
Teen: It's important!
Dad: Back then, we just called it "scrapbook glue and glitter."

Teen: Dad, I asked AI to tell me a joke about you.
Dad: Oh yeah? What'd it say?
Teen: "Error: Too many dad jokes detected."

Dad: I memorized multiplication tables.
Teen: I have a calculator app.
Dad: We called that "brain training," you call it "lazy efficiency."

Dad: We saved up for things we wanted.
Teen: I just use online payment plans.
Dad: And call it "instant gratification economics."

Dad: We actually had homework every night without Google.
Teen: Now I Google everything.
Dad: And call it "research." We called it "suffering."

Dad: We had to remember bus schedules.
Teen: I have an app.
Dad: And complain when it glitches. Same stress, just digital.

Dad: We played board games after school.
Teen: I play online games instead.
Dad: Same competition, fewer dice-related injuries.

Dad: We actually went to libraries.
Teen: I just Google everything.
Dad: And call it "modern wisdom."

Dad: You can't survive without your charger?
Teen Daughter: It's essential.
Dad: I survived for weeks on a single Nokia battery... and lots of patience.

Dad: You have 20 apps open at once?
Teen: Multitasking.
Dad: Back in my day, we called that "forgetting what we were doing halfway through homework."

Dad: You order food and complain it took 10 minutes?
Teen Daughter: Speed matters!
Dad: Back then, speed was running to the corner store before they closed.

Dad: You take selfies for 20 minutes?
Teen: It's an art form.
Dad: Back then, art was carving initials into a tree — fewer angles, more splinters.

Dad: You call texting a conversation?
Teen: It's the modern way.
Dad: Back in my day, conversations required a chair, vocal chords, and stamina.

Dad: You spend hours scrolling memes?
Teen Daughter: They're inspirational!
Dad: Back then, we just stared at our ceiling thinking deep thoughts.

Dad: You have 10 tabs open while doing homework?
Teen: Research!
Dad: Back then, research meant flipping pages and accidentally tearing the book.

Dad: You cancel plans because of weather?
Teen Daughter: It's called self-care.
Dad: Back then, weather was a challenge, not an excuse to stay in.

Dad: You've got Bluetooth earbuds in everywhere.
Teen: They're convenient.
Dad: Back then, "convenient" meant untangling a cord until someone lost their mind.

Dad: When I was your age, we played outside until dark.
Teen: Now I just play Fortnite until dark.
Dad: Same principle, slightly more screen glare.

Dad: You rely on Google Maps for every step?
Teen Daughter: It's efficient.
Dad: Back then, we just got lost and called it "adventure."

Dad: You can't remember a phone number.
Teen: I have a contacts list.
Dad: Back then, memory was a muscle — we exercised it constantly.

Dad: You swipe left and right for dating?
Teen: Modern dating.
Dad: Back then, you actually said hello in person — and maybe got slapped for it.

Dad: You spend hours editing videos?
Teen Daughter: It's creative!
Dad: Back then, "editing" meant erasing pencil mistakes — slower, but satisfying.

Dad: You're updating your status constantly.
Teen: It's life documentation.
Dad: We just had embarrassing yearbooks — same effect, less Wi-Fi.

Dad: You spend hours on skincare routines?
Teen Daughter: It's self-care.
Dad: Back then, soap and water were revolutionary

Dad: You skip meals because of homework?
Teen Daughter: Busy schedule!
Dad: Back then, we ate cereal for dinner and called it gourmet.

Dad: You have multiple chargers in your bag?
Teen: Backup, Dad.
Dad: Back then, "backup" was a pencil stub and a bad eraser.

Dad: You video call friends instead of meeting them?
Teen Daughter: Convenience!
Dad: Back then, convenience meant walking in the rain and hoping they were home.

Dad: You read fanfiction for hours?
Teen: It's storytelling!
Dad: Back then, our "fanfiction" was passing notes with doodles — riskier, but more thrill-ing.

Dad: You use a spell-checker for every text?
Teen Daughter: Accuracy matters.
Dad: Back then, mistakes were permanent. We called it "learning the hard way."

Dad: You check the weather constantly.
Teen: It's responsible.
Dad: Back then, clouds were all the info we needed — and wet socks were proof.

Dad: You worry about likes on every post?
Teen Daughter: Social validation matters.
Dad: Back then, validation was a smile from the neighbor — cheaper, and less dramatic.

Teen: Dad, I can make viral videos in minutes!
Dad: That's cool, but can you film, edit, and still survive a camping trip?
Teen Daughter: ...Now I see why survival skills are old-school

Teen: Why did the Wi-Fi get in trouble?
Dad: Why?
Teen: Because it couldn't connect with others.

Teen: Dad, you're like a software update.
Dad: Meaning I'm improving with age?
Teen: No, you pop up when I'm busy and take forever to finish.

Teen: I told Mom I'd help clean if I got a "thank you."
Dad: What'd she say?
Teen: She said, "Thank you in advance."

Teen: Dad, you're trending!
Dad: Really? On what platform?
Teen: The neighborhood social media group — for mowing in socks again.

Teen: Why did the phone go to therapy?
Dad: Why?
Teen: Too many "unresolved issues."

Teen: Dad, you remind me of a YouTube ad.
Dad: Because I'm everywhere?
Teen: Because I can't skip you.

Teen: Dad, can you transfer me $20?
Dad: What happened to saying "please"?
Teen: Inflation. It's $25 now.

Dad: Always keep a paper map in your car.
Teen: But I have GPS!
Dad: GPS dies. Paper doesn't. Welcome to the analog survival club.

Teen Daughter: Dad, I can take a great photo perfectly.
Dad: Can you also take a photo without dropping the camera?
Teen Daughter: ...Well, there's still room to improve.

Dad: I'll teach you how to fold a fitted sheet.
Teen: Isn't that impossible?
Dad: That's why it's called an "old trick." Consider it advanced ninja training.

Teen: Dad, I can Google everything!
Dad: Sure, but can Google start a fire, patch a tire, or fix a leaky tap at midnight?
Teen Daughter: ...Touché.

Dad: Let me show you how to make a campfire without matches.
Teen Daughter: Wait... why not just use a lighter?
Dad: Because someday you'll want bragging rights — and maybe a survival story.

Dad: You have to learn how to write a proper thank-you note.
Teen: But I can just text "Thanks lol."
Dad: Back then, we called handwriting a "life skill" — fewer emojis, more charm.

Dad: Always check the oil before a long trip.
Teen Daughter: I can just check the car app.
Dad: Apps lie. Mechanics don't. Also, you'll thank me when your car still runs.

Dad: You should know how to change a tire.
Teen: But Dad, I can call roadside assistance.
Dad: Sure, but then who gets the story credit? Skills > service.

Dad: Let me show you how to tie a proper knot.
Teen Daughter: But I have Velcro sneakers.
Dad: True, but someday you'll need it in the wild — or for embarrassing campfire stories.

Dad: It's midnight. Go to bed.
Teen: You're up too.
Dad: I'm a grown adult.
Teen: So you're saying adulthood is just being tired all the time?
Dad: ...Pretty much.

Dad: Who used up all the data?
Teen: You streamed three hours of golf highlights!
Dad: That's educational!
Teen: Only if I'm training to nap.

Dad: You're wearing that out in public?
Teen: Yeah, why?
Dad: Just wondering if I should walk ten steps behind or twenty.
Teen: Make it thirty — fashion doesn't wait for fear.

Dad: You're braking too late!
Teen: You said trust my instincts!
Dad: I didn't say trust them with my life!
Teen: Then stop yelling — I'm trying to focus on the GPS and your panic.

Dad: You know, laundry doesn't fold itself.
Teen: I was testing that theory.
Dad: And your results?
Teen: Promising. Still in the data-collection phase.

Dad: I cooked. You're welcome.
Teen: You mean you microwaved leftovers.
Dad: Still counts. Effort was applied.
Teen: Barely — even the microwave sighed.

Dad: Finally, real music — 80s rock!
Teen: Real music? They still used cassette tapes!
Dad: And talent.
Teen: And hairspray. Lots of hairspray.

Teen: I need a raise in my allowance.
Dad: Based on what performance metrics?
Teen: I exist in your house peacefully.
Dad: Debatable — we're still negotiating noise levels.

Teen: Dad, stop embarrassing me.
Dad: I can't. It's in the contract.
Teen: What contract?!
Dad: The one you signed when you were born — in drool.

Teen Daughter: You walked everywhere to hang out with friends.
Dad: Yep, and we survived.
Teen Daughter: Now I hop from place to place in minutes.
Dad: At least no one's getting mud in their shoes.

Teen: You had mixtapes for your crush.
Dad: Classic.
Teen: I have playlists with random songs.
Dad: Technology: making love awkward since... forever.

Teen Daughter: You read books for fun.
Dad: I did.
Teen Daughter: Now I read short stories and notes.
Dad: Somehow, I think your brain isn't getting the same exercise.

Teen: You memorized phone numbers.
Dad: True.
Teen: Now we just screenshot them.
Dad: And complain when the screenshot is blurry.

Teen Daughter: When you were my age, you walked to school uphill both ways?
Dad: Pretty much.
Teen Daughter: Now I just scroll uphill on my phone.
Dad: Same workout, less frostbite.

Teen: Dad, you can use shortcuts on the computer to work faster.
Dad: Shortcuts?
Teen: Yes — press a few keys instead of clicking everywhere.
Dad: Wow... I've been doing it the hard way for 20 years.

Teen Daughter: Dad, you can schedule reminders so you don't forget anything.
Dad: Reminders?
Teen Daughter: Yes — your brain can take a day off.
Dad: I feel like I've just been promoted to assistant.

Teen: Dad, you can copy text instead of rewriting it.
Dad: Copy?
Teen: Ctrl + C, Ctrl + V — instant perfection.
Dad: Incredible... and yet I've been losing at handwriting contests for years.

Teen Daughter: Dad, you can track your steps with a simple pedometer.
Dad: Track steps?
Teen Daughter: Yes, and know exactly how far you walked.
Dad: So my memory isn't failing — it's just unrecorded.

Teen: Dad, you can color-code your calendar to stay organized.
Dad: Color-code?
Teen: Yes — everything in its own category.
Dad: Suddenly my chaos looks like a masterpiece.

Teen Daughter: Dad, you can label cables so you don't unplug the wrong one.
Dad: Labels?
Teen Daughter: Yes — no more accidental blackouts.
Dad: Genius. My last mistake made me look like a mad scientist.

Teen: Dad, you can search for specific words in a document.
Dad: Search?
Teen: Yes — instant results.
Dad: My fingers thank you… they were tired from scrolling.

Teen Daughter: Dad, you can use sticky notes digitally.
Dad: Digital sticky notes?
Teen Daughter: Yep — reminders without clutter.
Dad: Finally... no more losing random scraps of paper.

Teen: Dad, you can automate simple tasks on the computer.
Dad: Automate?
Teen: Yes — let the tech do the boring stuff.
Dad: Incredible... my laziness just got upgraded.

Teen Daughter: Dad, you can draw diagrams to understand anything faster.
Dad: Draw diagrams?
Teen Daughter: Visual learning is easier.
Dad: So my scribbles actually have a purpose.

Teen: Dad, you're so out of touch.
Dad: Maybe. But I've seen enough trends come and go to know this one will too.
Teen: You're saying my style's temporary?
Dad: No, I'm saying you'll figure out what's really you.

Teen: You don't get what it's like to be a teenager!
Dad: You'd be surprised. I just had worse hair and no Wi-Fi.
Teen: So you're saying it was harder back then?
Dad: No, just different — every generation has its own kind of hard.

Teen: Ugh, you're always checking on me.
Dad: That's how you know I care. When I stop asking — worry.
Teen: You're not gonna stop, are you?
Dad: Not a chance. Love's kind of a lifetime subscription.

Teen: You always have to have the last word!
Dad: That's not true...
Teen: See?!
Dad: (smiles) Okay, fine — you get this one. I'll still be right later.

Teen: You're always making jokes about me.
Dad: Only because I think you're awesome.
Teen: That's... weird logic.
Dad: Nah — it's called "parenting with personality."

Teen: You never let me do anything!
Dad: I let you do plenty — I just try to keep you out of trouble.
Teen: You think I'd mess up?
Dad: I think I did — and I'm trying to help you skip a few of my mistakes.

Teen: Why do you always lecture me?
Dad: Because I've already paid for the lessons.
Teen: You mean with experience?
Dad: No — with dumb choices and car repairs.

Teen: You're so strict, Dad.
Dad: I'm not strict, I'm invested.
Teen: That sounds the same.
Dad: It does — until you have your own teenager someday.

Teen: You act like you know everything.
Dad: Nah, I just remember what it's like to think I did.
Teen: That's not funny.
Dad: It wasn't back then either — but I laugh now.

Teen: You're always making fun of me.
Dad: Only because I love you.
Teen: That's a weird way to show it.
Dad: Yeah — but someday, you'll laugh at it too.

Teen: You can use filters to make your photo look better.
Dad: Filters?
Teen: Yes, it's like Photoshop in your pocket.
Dad: So my bad hair day just became... slightly less tragic.

Teen: Dad, you can pin apps to your home screen.
Dad: Pin apps?
Teen: It's faster.
Dad: Back in my day, we pinned things with actual pins... to corkboards.

Teen Daughter: Dad, you can make a funny caption on a photo in seconds.
Dad: Caption?
Teen Daughter: Yes — text + picture = instant humor.
Dad: And yet somehow, my jokes still take longer to understand.

Teen Daughter: Dad, you can use voice-to-text on your phone.
Dad: Voice-to-text?
Teen Daughter: Just talk.
Dad: Amazing... it types exactly what I don't want to say.

Teen: Dad, you have to swipe up to see the full story.
Dad: Swipe up?
Teen: Yep. Modern magic.
Dad: And here I thought "magic" was misplacing the remote.

Teen: You read newspapers.
Dad: True.
Teen: I scroll headlines online.
Dad: Quick, but somehow you still miss the weird stuff.

Teen Daughter: You didn't have a selfie stick.
Dad: Nope.
Teen Daughter: I have a tripod and ring light.
Dad: At least your arms don't cramp... just your patience.

Teen: You had to remember friends' birthdays.
Dad: Yep.
Teen: I get Facebook reminders.
Dad: Convenient, but slightly less heartfelt.

Teen Daughter: You learned songs on cassette radios.
Dad: Yep.
Teen Daughter: I stream on playlists.
Dad: Same music, zero static.

Teen: You wrote essays by hand.
Dad: Yep.
Teen: I type and auto-save.
Dad: Same effort, zero ink smudges.

Teen Daughter: You actually hung out in malls for fun.
Dad: Yep, just walking and talking.
Teen Daughter: I scroll online stores instead.
Dad: And call it "retail therapy in pajamas."

Teen: You walked everywhere to hang out.
Dad: Yep.
Teen: I Uber or call them on video.
Dad: You still got shoes on, so some progress.

Teen Daughter: You made phone calls to apologize.
Dad: True.
Teen Daughter: I just send memes.
Dad: Humor: the modern apology method.

Teen: You had mixtapes for crushes.
Dad: Classic.
Teen: I make playlists with algorithms.
Dad: At least your crush doesn't have to untangle a cassette.

Teen Daughter: You actually talked in person to friends.
Dad: Every day.
Teen Daughter: Now we just DM.
Dad: Same friendship, less awkward breathing.

Teen: You actually called friends on the phone?
Dad: Yep.
Teen: I just text.
Dad: Same outcome — arguments about nothing included.

Teen Daughter: You wrote notes in class.
Dad: True.
Teen Daughter: I take screenshots.
Dad: Efficient, but nostalgia doesn't screenshot.

Teen: You went outside to find out gossip?
Dad: Yep, neighbors and the corner store.
Teen: Now I scroll Insta stories.
Dad: Faster, but slightly less juicy.

Teen Daughter: You wore jeans until they ripped.
Dad: And patched them.
Teen Daughter: I buy ripped jeans new.
Dad: Fashion innovation or laziness? You decide.

Teen: You had to pay for everything in cash.
Dad: Yep.
Teen: Now I just tap my card and forget.
Dad: Future accountants everywhere are crying.

Teen Daughter: You sent actual letters.
Dad: True.
Teen Daughter: I just send GIFs and emojis.
Dad: Efficient… but less papercuts.

Teen: You had landlines.
Dad: True.
Teen: I have unlimited texting.
Dad: Same job, easier to hang up on people.

Teen Daughter: You said you wrote in diaries.
Dad: Yeah, every night.
Teen Daughter: Now I tweet my feelings.
Dad: At least no one steals your diary — but the internet remembers forever.

Dad: You kids have it easy.
Teen: Really? You cry over slow Wi-Fi.
Dad: That's different — it's life or death!
Teen: Yeah, you definitely survived tougher times.

Dad: I was a straight-A student.
Teen: In what century?
Dad: Watch it, kid.
Teen: Sorry, ancient scholar.

Dad: You'll understand when you're older.
Teen: That's what you said about taxes.
Dad: And?
Teen: Still waiting, still confused.

Teen: You actually had friends over to talk?
Dad: Yep.
Teen: Now I just send voice notes.
Dad: And we call it socializing... less sweaty.

Dad: You're always on that phone!
Teen: And you're always on the weather app.
Dad: That's called being informed.
Teen: I call it rain anxiety.

Dad: You don't know how good you've got it.
Teen: Oh, I know — I've got unlimited data.
Dad: And who pays for that?
Teen: My biggest fan. Thanks, Dad.

Dad: I don't like your tone.
Teen: It's called sarcasm — it's a teen language.
Dad: Well, I don't speak it.
Teen: You do. Every time you say "nice room."

Dad: You should get a job and learn responsibility.
Teen: I already have one.
Dad: Doing what?
Teen: Managing your mood swings.

Teen: Dad, you can't dance. Please stop.
Dad: I'm not dancing — I'm emotionally expressing my rhythm.
Teen: It looks like a cramp.
Dad: That's just how legends move, kid.

Teen: You never take me seriously!
Dad: I do — except when you say, "I'll be ready in five minutes."
Teen: I mean it this time!
Dad: I'll start the timer... in half an hour.

Teen: You don't understand fashion, Dad.
Dad: True — I wear comfort like a badge of honor.
Teen: That's not a trend.
Dad: It is when you stop caring what strangers think.

Teen: Why do you always tell dad jokes?
Dad: Because you react every time.
Teen: I'm not reacting!
Dad: Mission accomplished.

Teen: You're too old to be cool, Dad.
Dad: That's fine — I was cool before it was cool to be cool.
Teen: That makes zero sense.
Dad: Exactly. That's how you know it's wisdom.

Teen: You're so dramatic.
Dad: And yet, somehow, you're the one who sighs like it's a Shakespeare play.
Teen: You're impossible.
Dad: That's "Dad" to you.

Dad: You know, I used to be cool.
Teen: Used to be?
Dad: Yeah, before parenting happened.
Teen: Don't worry — you're still cool... for Wi-Fi support.

Dad: When I was your age, we respected our parents.
Teen: When you were my age, dinosaurs respected you too.
Dad: Funny.
Teen: Thanks, must be genetic.

Teen: Dad, why do you always make lame jokes?
Dad: Because one day, you'll steal them and call them funny.
Teen: Never gonna happen.
Dad: That's exactly what I said to my dad.

Teen: You always embarrass me in public!
Dad: Oh, don't worry — I save my best material for school events.
Teen: Dad, no!
Dad: Relax, I'll only wave if your friends are watching.

Teen: You think you're funny, huh?
Dad: No, I know I'm funny — it's genetic.
Teen: From who?
Dad: Your grandma — she roasted me before it was cool.

Teen: You don't even know what "slay" means!
Dad: Sure I do. It's what I do to lawns every weekend.
Teen: That's not— okay, fine, you win.
Dad: As usual.

Dad: Smile for a family photo!
Teen: I just did.
Dad: You blinked.
Teen: That's called being alive, Dad.
Dad: Not in my camera roll it isn't.